Here I am in the middle of the Covid 19 lockdown with time on my hands.

I promised everyone that one day I would write this

very book.

I have been writing a blog for many years and so many of the taxi tales are in there.

www.dublintaxi.blogspot.com

So if you enjoy it tell all your friends

If you don't like it, save your breath.

G000081149

Here we go, buckle up

THE CYCLONE COURIER

I picked up Rasheed with his wife and 2 kids one day, his wife was from Hungary and he was Pakistani. His wife had the most amazing green eyes, they were like the eyes of a red haired Irish girl..

So I drove them to their house and he picked up a small bag and I drove him to the airport.

He told me that he was training to become a pilot in Sarajevo and he was putting himself through it all by riding a bicycle for the Cyclone courier company.

Fair play to him. I hoped that he would make it through.

I met him after that in Harcourt St and he had progressed to the next level.

I was amazed by how well he was doing, the next time we met he had passed all the exams and all he had to do was to put in flying hours. He went to South Africa where he flew air freight.

Now he is a fully qualified pilot.

So the next time you fly on Pakistan airways you might

find yourself in the very capable hands of Rasheed.

It took some great determination to do all that by delivering packages on a bicycle.

AN EDUCATION THROUGH A THOUSAND JOURNEYS

TO DRIVE A TAXI YOU HAVE TO HAVE A PSV LISCENCE
Public Service Vehicle licence.

So I went into the Garda station in Kevin St.

I went up to the hatch and told him that I wanted a form to be vetted for the PSV licence.

Where's your P45?(Details of unemployment form)

I am on a 3 day week and by the time this comes through I will be unemployed. So I won't have my P45 till then.

Next! He shouted, dismissing me.

I am not finished I said.

Next! He said again glaring into my face.

A friend of mine gave back his taxi plate to this Garda station a few months ago and he found that the Garda that took it in has transferred it into his own name.

Two other Garda have taxis rented out.

Where is their P45?

'You are a very awkward man' he said picking up the form.

Then he stamped it and gave it to me.

(I only give you this to show what friction existed between some Garda and taxi drivers)

A few months later I got the all clear.

I had been out of work for 3 weeks at that time.

So I sat the taxi driving exam and became driver C1313.

There was a limit to the number of taxis at that time.

No new taxi plates were being issued.

If you wanted to buy a taxi you had to find one where the owner had died.

The London cabby called it "Dead men's shoes"

I tried to rent a taxi but the guys who had them wanted to lay down the law very much on their terms.

You have to take Monday Tuesday off and there were 100 other little things you had to do for them.

I wanted Wed. Thursday off as I knew that Monday was a busy day back then.

The next alternative was to have your family car passed out as a Hackney car and work on the radio from a base.

Then after a while looking I went to Metro, a radio cab company.

The customer called for a cab by phone and the base man passed you the message and the customer was then charged by the mile- .No taxi meter.

Then one day around 18 months later I must have said something to the base man at some stage and he cut off my oxygen supply, I got bad jobs and the guys behind me started getting the work instead of me.

So I slung my hook and abandoned ship and gave it up.

Some time later, I saw a Fiat Scudo wheelchair taxi for sale in the Evening Herald for £12,000 !

I couldn't understand why it was so cheap, but the guy selling it told me that the taxi plate numbers had been de regulated.

Boys oh boys the numbers in Dublin went from 2,500 taxis in Dublin or so to over 12,000 in a few years

Even in New York city at that time the taxi numbers were not as high as 12,000.

In Ireland the value of the taxi plate went from £90,000 down to £2,500, now they are non- transferable and so they a have no re-sale value.

In New York the cost of a taxi licence (medallion) went from over $1 million to nothing.

Uber had hit NewYork and they treated the drivers with some respect unlike the taxi garages, so the drivers defected away from the Yellow Cabs.

There was a bit of dog eat dog here in Dublin for a while, with so many taxis.

 You had to work longer hours for the same money etc.

Then a strange thing came along called Hailo!

It worked by app through the modern mobile phone.

The customer pressed the screen of his phone and the driver knew where the customer was. No base man.

It also allowed the customer to pay by credit card.

The cost to the driver was 5% Then it went up to10% then 12% and now to 15%

When Hailo started, the front line office was run by taxi drivers and they knew what we as taxi drivers were dealing with and there was mutual respect.

Now front line staff who work there are 20 year olds who have no respect at all for the taxi drivers.

So I will get on with a few stories I picked up along the road.

THE WILD VIXEN

Harcourt St. had quite a few wild venues, and I picked up this sly vixen one night going to Glasneven.(A Vixen is a female fox)

She hopped into the 6 seater and lay down on the back seat.

As I was coming up on to Dorset St. she bolted up from her seat.

"Help! Help! I've been kidnapped"

There was a button you could hold down to prevent children from opening the doors. I slowed way down and told her that she had voluntarily got into the taxi and I was taking her to Glasneven. She put her hand into her crotch and started to shout RAPE!

You bastard !

I told her that we would go to Whitehall Garda station.'

If you take me to the Garda you will lose your licence and you will be locked up as a sexual predator! Your kids going to school will be pointed at and your wife will kick you out.

But if you give me £300 I will let it go.'

'Well ,Well, if only life was so simple' I said.

"What are you on about, you scumbag."

Sometimes its not just' He said, She said.'

They will take a sample from you.
Then there is the little matter of the video camera over
your head.
I turned on the light and she saw it.

When she saw it she just said.
Oh well in that case you can just take me home.
They were outside the Whitehall Garda station at that
point and I blew the horn 6 or 7 times.
No response, but I got paid and off she went, I often
wish that I had the bottle to grab her by the hair of her
head and drag her in.
I went in myself and there was a Garda behind the glass
and he refused to get involved.

'Sure if you didn't pay her no crime was comitted'.

OLD JIMMY

When I worked for Metro we used to meet at night at the Spar shop in Baggott st.

There we would exchange tales of the unexpected.

One guy, lets call him Jimmy ,he was retired and very careful with money.

He made sandwiches for his shift and he had a flask.

He was a nice guy, loved to talk and this was his hobby, tai driving !.

It took him out of the house.

So it came as a big surprise to learn that he had paid for his grandson and family to go to Disneyland Florida.He kept his personal life very much to himself but the other guys "Soft Soaped" him and the story leaked out.

Instructions on the radio were causing him friction, he couldn't write down the instructions fast enough and he panicked which made things worse.

Then his grandson gave him an early Christmas present.

Everything was going fine after that, instructions taken in an instant, it was great for him.

One day he got a job to Castleknock and when he reached there was a fare of £18 on the sheet. Here is £20 she will pay you the balance when you get to Cabra.

On arrival in Cabra he asked for £2

"Ya got £20 it's enough for you".

I am not a charity he said.

If you don't pay me I will bring you to the Garda station.

She got then really agressive.

Look at me you stupid bollix If you bring me to the Garda station I will scratch my face and tear my clothes and tell them that you tried to rape me and you will lose your licence.

So he drove to the Garda station and he stopped the car and watched her punch and scratch her face and then she ran into the Garda station with blouse torn and her breasts exposed.

He went to the back of the car and got his coat, locking the car he went in to face the firing squad.

"There he is the bastard! Look at what he did to me."

"Arrest that man" said the Garda

Have you no sense lads said Jimmy, would I bring her here if I had done all that.

Do you want to hear my side of the story?.

Or should I say. Her side of the story.

He produced a small Dictaphone and pressed play.

He had it all..

The girl fainted.

When she was came around he asked for and got his £2

She was under the legal age and her parents were called for, they had to listen to the recording.

What a punishment for the poor parents.

When he went back the next day to collect his Dictaphone the Garda apologised to him and said that they would be keeping a good eye on that girl in future.

They also said that it was a big wake up call for them, without the tape they would have believed her, not him.

So Jimmy went to the travel agent and to reward his grandson for the useful Christmas present he gave his son's family the holiday of a lifetime, he sent them to Disneyland Florida

THE BOUNCER

No book worth its salt about taxi driving would not mention bouncers.

The guys that can really spoil your day.

So a taxi driver and his wife went into town for a movie, after the movie the taxi driver wanted to get on the bus and go home and have a pint in the local pub. His wife wanted to go to one of the city pubs and then take a taxi home.

So they approached a well known city pub and the bouncer stopped them. "It's locals only tonight. Nothing personal. But not tonight"

His wife said Its OK Tony we can get a bus home.

So 3 weeks later the skies opened and the rain came lashing down at pub -closing time.

The taxi rank at the top of Grafton was 50 deep.

Tony was flying and a guy jumped in, Finglas he said.

Tony said to him as he drove away. "Your face is familiar, where do I know you from?"

I work the doors !

Bang! Tony hit the brakes.

Sorry mate its regulars only tonight.

I hope you are not offended, perhaps another night.

This other one happened to me.

He got in and said Rathfarnham.

He was really gloomy so I said .

"Who stole the cherry off your bun?"

Is it that obvious? he said.

So I will tell you the whole story, from beginning until right now.

My parents had a pub and when we were of college age they were killed in a car crash. My brother and I ran the business and when we were older we decided that we liked the pub business. One pub could not support 2 families. So we took out a loan on one pub and bought a second pub.

The girl upstairs ran the office, the ordering of stock etc., then we bought more pubs until we had 12 pubs between us and a wholesale business.

I said that was really great.

A friend of ours bought a pub and when he renovated it, with all the work done with the delays and extra expenses he had run out of money.

So I decided to buy a share in the pub with like 6 months or more of stock.

The place was doing really badly.

I sent my son in to see what was going on, he told me tht everything was fine, but it was quiet.

So tonight I went to take a look for myself.

I was playing with my fone as I approached the pub when I felt a hand on my arm.

Sorry sir you can't go in, it's regulars only.

Give me a proper reason why I cannot go in.

He looked me in the eye and said.

"Fuck off Grandad"

I got really annoyed, I rang Sam the guy who owns the company that deals with security at all my pubs.

"I am standing outside my pub and YOUR bouncer will not let me in. Please sack him and his pal. I will see you in my office on Tuesday"

The pub took in more money that night than they had in the previous fortnight.

He was of the opinion that the bouncers were working for a rival pub.

No I said those guys have got power and they just love to use it.

RETIREMENT

So he got into the taxi and I could feel that he was fuming about something.

"Do you want to talk about something? "I asked.

'When I was a young lad I loved engineering and I went to college and later I worked for a few big companies.

I went out on my own and cornered a niche market and I found great people to work with me.

Not for me, but with me. There is a hell of a difference in those 2 words.

I was heading for 60 and I had planned to retire at 60.

So one day a very large American company found me and they made me an offer I could not refuse, so I sold the company to them.

One provision was that I would work with them for a year to bed them in, to show them where the pencils were kept etc.

They are great at holding meetings, producing graphs, studying market trends etc.

I was at one meeting and I asked everyone to stop and to take out a pad of paper and to name six people who held key roles in the company, I told them what they did, how those people fitted into the company etc. they didn't name one.

I was frustrated and next thing was that my best technician came to me and said he was leaving.

This guy spots trouble before it happens, he is one of a kind..

Why are you going ? I asked him.

I offered him a 50% pay rise, but he said no.

He explained that the new workers in the company were very hard to deal with.

'They don't ask me if I see any problem in what they are doing, they just say do this, do that.

So I am leaving. The first company I rang up gave me a job'.

'The guys in suits think that they can replace him with a new college graduate, but 20 years experience does not come cheap.'

The company went on to regret the technician's departure as they were soon floundering.

Then he went on to say;

A client of mine who dresses like a hippie came in to my office the other day to get some work done and I took him to Durty Nellies for lunch. He was shocked to hear that I had sold the company and he asked me to work with him and a few big hitters on his project in Africa.

A few years ago this same hippie had pulled a massive

prank on me.

He had arrived into my office out of the blue with an American guy and the three of us went to lunch. We talked business. The American seemed to know a lot about technology. I asked him what line of business he was in himself. My hippie friend just laughed at the good of it.

'Let me introduce you to Bill Gates!'

If you saw this hippie. you would think that he was broke, but he is a multi billionaire, he is funding a project in Africa and saving thousands of lives in the process.

Because he is using his own money he also attracts a lot of other finance to his cause.

After the lunch was over, we arrived back at the office of my company and the new secretary ungraciously handed him the bill for the work done, without a word.

She never even addressed him by name.

I felt ashamed at her behaviour.

That poorly dressed hippie would give away in one month more money than most people would make in their entire lives.

She couldn't see past his torn jeans.

Then he went on to say;

I got a phone call yesterday from head office asking me to work with them for a second year.

What do you think of that?

So I gave him my tuppence worth.

'Tell them the truth, they are killing the company. Tell them you have other plans.

So the next big thing on his agenda was to go and visit his sister in the USA and then on to Australia after that,perhaps golf, or learn how to sail.

THE GOLFER

He got into the taxi on Dawson St and was heading to the airport. He was amazed by the dashboard of the Prius. It has an electric motor and a petrol engine I explained this to him and he really was charmed by the technology.

What do you do yourself? I asked.

I have just turned professional he said.

Professional at what? I said

I'm a golfer.

I have just now signed a contract to turn professional.

Congratulations I said. I hope it goes really well for you. When you reach the top level it is the person who has the best concentration who wins.

I am only part of a team he said, I have all kinds of managers to keep my mind in focus.

Any more advice for me ?

This might seem to be strange, be generous with your time and your money, people appreciate that. So I asked his name, just so I could look out for him.

Rory, Rory McIlroy.

You know he has done well for himself, plus he has given millions to charity.

A sports writer who lives in Furry Park in Clontarf was going to do an interview with him years after we met and he took my photo at the airport. He put the photo on his facebook and told the story of how I had met Rory on the first day he turned professional.

He showed the photo that he had taken of me at the airport and Rory still remembered me.

CHELTENHAM

There was a businessman in the midlands who was doing well, he had a passion for racing and instead of taking his staff out at Christmas to celebrate, he opted instead to take his entire staff off for a weeks racing at Cheltenham.

It was the climax of their year.

Then there was an outbreak of foot and mouth disease one year and the race meeting was cancelled.

Every year when they were going home he paid for all the food and drink they had consumed that year and then paid for the next year's hotel bill to reserve it.

So he rang the hotel and said that he was not coming this year, but to carry over the booking until the following year.

The hotel said that the booking was non transferable. He would have to pay again next time .

He was gobsmacked. But what could he do?

He had a brother who was a priest and he explained the situation to him and they worked out a plan.

The priest hired a minibus and filled it with homeless people and arrived at the hotel.

There was quite an argument, but the priest insisted that they were coming for the week as arranged. The hotel finally relented and gave back the money. The Irish businessman told his brother that it was an awful shock to his system to find how little they had appreciated his business.

That money went to help the poor in the parish and the following year they found another hotel in which to enjoy the races.

CHUCK FEENEY

As long as I live I will remember this man.

I picked him and his wife at the airport and brought them to The Berkley Court hotel in Ballsbridge.

'If I was starting my life again I would love to be a taxi driver' he said.

'It's not all sunshine you know' I said.

'You can come and go as you please, you are your own boss and you don't have to put up with bad manners.' So I gave him an example of a bad customer I had in the taxi the other day and he said.

'You handled it all wrong. You should have stopped the car and told them to get out.'

I did that 3 times since then, normally a warning checks them but the second guy was so surprised that he offered me £100 on top of the taxi fare if I brought him to the airport.

'No' I said, ' money can't buy your way out of this'. He started to cry like a spoiled child as I drove away.

Anyhow to get back to the story.

He spoke to me about work-life balance,

The importance of setting out a plan and then rewarding yourself when you reach your goal.

It is very important to live within your means.

If you earn € 1,000 a week that is your budget, save a little bit,don't spend more money than you have.

People who live on their credit cards might have to work ten or 20 years longer just to clear their debts. If you needed a new engine for the taxi then you might have to go into debt..

Work hard and pay it off straight away.

Make a list of things that you have to do.

I bet you have something outstanding to do?

Yes my income tax.

When is it due? Next month, in 3 weeks

How much have you done?

Nothing!

You see this kind of thing drains your energy.

Make a list and do 2 of the hardest things first every week

Tell your kids to look after their own retirement, buy small amounts of shares in different companies every 1/4, build your own portfolio. If you manage it yourself you will do far better than some of these experts handling your money. By the time they take their fees every year you would be lucky to get your initial investment back.

As a taxi driver at least 3 great ideas will pass your ear

every month.

All you have to do is to catch one of them and use it yourself.

Then the interrogation started

What did you do before driving a taxi?

So I gave him a quick recap. of my career.

'You have had an interesting and varied life so far.

What else are you working at now?'

'I started a business called "The ink elephant" Refilling ink cartridges'

'Where did you come across that idea?'.

In Boston, a company called Staples

How is it going ? Are you having problems?

Yes the inks we are getting are not consistent, they blot or block the jets, we are dealing with an Italian company and they are hopeless.

He was quiet for 2 minutes, Contact a company called Coates, they make dyes and inks. Contact Staples again as well just to run your idea past them again.

All this effort that you put into this is not wasted time; it is experience which will be useful in the future.

When we contacted Staples they told me that they had stopped doing it as the generic cartridges had come in now and the people who were getting cartridges re-filled would take them home, print a heap of work and then say that the cartridge must have been faulty.

Plus it was all email now.

So the Ink Elephant died

So he knew all about me and I knew nothing about him.

He asked me if I would come and work with him. He would be sending people over to Ireland and he wanted me to show them around, look after them.

 He would provide a good car for the purpose.

I said that I had to bring the kids to school in the morning and to cook the dinner in the evening.

Oh yes, look after your family first.

At the hotel he asked me to come in for coffee, but 9.30 is a busy time, so I declined his offer.

On Saturday I bought the Irish Times and there inside was a full page story about my passenger.

"It now can be revealed that the person behind Atlantic Philanthropies is none other than Chuck Feeney"

I have carried that name in my heart for more than 15 years.

There is a book written about him.

"The Billionaire who wasn't " by Conor O'Cleary (I think it is out in Kindle)

Mr Feeney was always a wheeler dealer.

He was conscripted into the army and fought in Korea, when he got out he got an education in Cornell university where he studied hotel management, then he got a job selling Perfume and Brandy to American sailors coming in and out of Marseilles.

He had an idea one day and this idea defined the rest of his life.

He invented duty free shopping DFS. Look for it as you pass through the airport.

He never flashed the cash and lived a most frugal lifestyle.

He wears a $10 watch and I am sure he has just one good suit, but he doesn't dress to impress.

Instead of boasting about his great wealth he used it to help the people around the world, quietly.

He built Limerick University secretly.

Shannon was a very important location in his empire.

He gave millions away quietly to all the universities in Ireland.

During the Vietnam war he gave scholarships to thousands of poor kids so they could go to university instead of going to Vietnam.

Education is a big thing for him. Also research into Cancer, and lately he funded an entire study into Alzheimer's.

So get his book.

One story that pulls at the heart strings is about a visit he made to Vietnam.

He saw the utter devastation after the war and said

The Vietnamese people deserve more than this.

I am going away but I will come back soon when I work out what I can do"

So he arrived back a few months later with a team of experts.

I am going to build a hospital he said. These people are geologists, architects and builders'

So a few weeks he was back over to see the location of the hospital.

He approved the location and they started work.

There were delays in getting the work underway and Feeney was impatient to get things going.

'Get 4 portacabins and put them over there out of the way and have clinics, then as the hospital becomes available move into it bit by bit.'

The foundations were taking shape when he came back and people were being looked after. There was a young girl aged around 10 years old in great pain, stooped over with her arms held up covering her face.

'That poor child looks to be in terrible back-pain' he said.

'Her problem is much worse than that' the doctor said. Her face has been burned by Napalm and her skull is growing. The burned skin will not stretch. We are cutting the skin to relieve the pressure and allow her skull to grow. When she stops growing the surgeons will give her a new face, she is too young to be given strong pain killers

How could anyone do that to a child? said Chuck, at least we are doing something.

So 6 years or so later the hospital was working well and someone said.

Let's have a proper opening for the hospital!

Good idea, next Wednesday get every priest from every religion to come and bless every corner of the hospital and then my wife will cut the ribbon.

(I believe that it is a 200 bed hospital, not a small clinic)

The ribbon was cut and a young girl stepped forward with a bunch of flowers.

They went for a light meal with the hospital administrator. During the meal Chuck asked the administrator how the little girl with the burned face had turned out.

Oh I'm sorry! Did no one tell you? That was the girl who gave your wife the flowers.

There was no pain in her face, no scars, just a radiant beautiful and happy teenager.

He did not bring her back to look at her.

He looked at his wristwatch as he spoke.

 This wristwatch cost me $10.

I got a year's warranty on the battery, It keeps perfect time.

But people I know would spend three times the total cost of fixing her life on just a wrist watch.

It's up to them. But I know where to get good value for

my money.

He was equally generous in Ireland.

He went into the department of education once and said ,

"I have £12 million and I want it to be used for research and development in computer science.

But you must match it with equal funding"

The excuses came how things were bad and the department couldn't come up with that kind of money.

So he came up with a good plan.

I have spoken to the UK government and they told me that they could come up with the money.

So you have until the 22nd of the month, or the money goes to the UK.

Because of that first big investment Microsoft had the graduates to open here in Europe.

I asked a guy from Atlantic once how Chuck Feeney knew that computers would be so big? After all, back then computers were just a green dot on a screen.

We didn't know.. We go to the pond with our bag of crumbs and we throw them into the pond. Some sink, a fish might get a crumb or a duck..

But sometimes a Swan comes along and we all just marvel at how wonderful life is.

I wrote to him to tell him how impressed I was about his story and I have stayed in touch with him right through the years.

I got a wonderful email of thanks for my input when they were closing down Atlantic.

Then one day an friend rang me.

I am just back from San Francisco. I was having dinner with an old friend of mine and he put down his fork and asked me if by any chance that I knew you, by name?

I nearly choked, Paul, do you know everyone in the world?

Not really I said, only the good ones.

So on the very day I picked him up I was driving him in to Dublin for a press conference.

Mr Obama had passed a new law.

You could not give away more than $2,000 anonymously so he had to declare what he had done with his wealth. The logic in this new law was to find who was making political donations to which political party.

I think you should be allowed to donate money to any honest cause you want to without anyone knowing.

Chuck gave away more than $8 billion dollars.

He has given more than e1.5 Billion to Ireland alone

So when I win the Euromillions I will make a call to him, just to find out how to keep it quiet.

THE ORPHAN

He got in at the Westbury hotel and he told me his story in the 15 minute journey. He was Irish though living in the USA since he was 13.

I was raised in an orphanage here in Ireland until I was adopted by a German couple who brought me to the USA.

I came back here and went to the orphanage to see if I could find out anything about my parents. I said "You were a brave man to do that!'

'I wish someone had told me that before I went' he said.

'When I saw the Orphanage, I collapsed on the ground, my heart pounding wildly. My wife and daughter thought I was having a heart attack. It was as if three big men were standing on my chest. It took me nearly an hour to regain my composure.

The nuns could give me no information, so that was a waste of time for me.

Can you imagine what it was like to reach the age of 13 and never to have been hugged or loved ?

The German couple taught me the German work ethic and with the charm of the Irish I made my way in the world. I worked as a carpenter. Another guy and I bought a run down house and we did it up and sold it again, after 10 or 12 times doing it we kept a house and lived in it for a while.

Later on we sold that house and bought a house each.

We went our separate ways. Then I found a niche market.

I fit out offices and now I operate in most of the states in America and in Europe as well.

I had an idea and I told him about it.

'I saw an article in the paper about orphans in Russia.

Whe they are 18 they are just turned out without any support. Pimps wait for the girls and "Employers" of a dubious type pick up the boys.

If you bought a house and took on boys who are in danger of going astray, you could train them up to be tradesmen. Create a safe environment for them.'

"Good idea" he said.

We had arrived at Guinnesses and he handed me £40.

You have to bring my wife and daughter back to the hotel.

I drove them back and I told his wife that I hoped he got some answers.

She said that he was a very strong man.

Back at the hotel I stopped the meter. There was £26 on the clock . I will get you the change' I said.

No Paul, whatever he gave you it's yours.

Some time later, I found his company through the

internet and the charity it supports is a charity called "Shoes for orphans"

He was lucky and not bitter about his past.

He is one of the really good guys.

THE GALWAY RACES

That week we had the super Galway races, a wonderful occasion for one and all.

Two taxi drivers decided to take a bit of time off and they drove the long road to Galway.

They had hot tips and blankets to spend the night in the car.

Coming home they were in a sorry state, they had lost all their money and they also had dreadful hangovers.

As they joined the long snake of traffic heading for the N4, a time of narrow roads and no motorways they were in despair. A young guy with a long coat was up ahead with his thumb up so they stopped.

When he got in he told them that this was the best Galway races he had had for years.

They moaned and groaned about their losses, he told them never to follow the horses.

He made them laugh with his jokes and stories and just when they had forgotten all their problems they were stopped by a Garda in Kilbeggan."You only have one headlamp working" on closer inspection he found a tax disc out of date and a bald tyre. When he inspected the driver's licence it was found to be a year out of date. Out came the notebook and pencil and the officer started writing and taking notes about everything.

When he had finished the passenger got out and went over to the Garda. He put his arm around him and patted him on the chest, he pulled the tail end of his uniform and said what fine men the boys in the car were.
' You should give them a chance.'

No! No! No! the Garda said so the hitch hiker then patted him on the chest again while the men in the car felt that they would all be locked up. He gave up and got back into the car.
"Lads I don't know what I was thinking about, the traffic is very heavy on this road, take a left here and I know a quicker route back to Dublin"
As they approached Crumlin in the early hours of the morning the hitchhiker pointed out where he wanted to get off.
"Don't worry about that Garda lads and his summons, unless he has a fantastic memory you are home and dry. That tunic of his was very tightly buttoned and I nearly didn't get it, but I managed it in the end.
I am a pickpocket, one of the best. Here's the Garda's notebook and that is why we went cross country, in case we were being chased.

I might see you at the races next year".

THE ACTUARY

He jumped into the car going to Foxrock and after the first few words I asked him what he did for a living.

I am an actuary, do you know what that is?.

Would it be a cross between a bookmaker and an undertaker? I asked.

He laughed.

"Not wrong there

My father was a bookie and he made me what I am today.

If he had a proper education he would have been a professor in Cambridge university.

When I was 10 he started to bring me to the races with him and showed me how to forecast the odds. At first I did not understand it.

But I soon copped on.

He would have me walk along and look at what the odds were on the other bookies' boards.

Later on we used a small child's walkie talkie to communicate. It was fun and I was learning mathematics by osmosis.

My Dad carried money and when he would go from one race meeting to another he would have a big bag full of money, so he bought a revolver, just in case.

One day when he had come back after being away for 2

days he counted out his cash in the sitting-room before he went to bank it.

The news came on in the kitchen and he went in to get the headlines. When he came back into the sitting room, the woman next door was talking to my mother in the hall.

As quick as you could say stop, he grabbed the neighbour by the hair and dragged her back into the sitting room".

'Put the money back on the table' he shouted as he pulled out the revolver.

My mother thought Dad had gone mad. She rang the police and told them that Dad was holding a neighbour hostage with a gun.

So three excited Gardai arrived at the house.

Fair play to Dad, he took control of the situation. He shouted 'PUT the money back on the table. She denied that she had taken any.

' I have to go to the loo' she said.

 Dad said' piss on the floor', then one of the Gardai tried to rush Dad.

He fired the gun at the ceiling and said

"You have 5 seconds before I shoot you.

One, Two, Three, Are you ready?"

OK she said pulling up her skirts and she drew out a wad of money.

The Garda grabbed Dad and the neighbour said. That's my money ! .

'Well here are the serial numbers of all the top notes in each pile, how do you explain that?'

They took my Dad and her away, later they searched her house and found property belonging to all the neighbours.

The judge let off my dad but he took away his gun licence.
He worked way past his 70s.
 All his kids were great mathematicians.

He died last year and each one of us used to spend 2 nights of the week with him while he was dying. It was not sad, we just talked with him and went over old times.
I said to him one night that I used to steal money from the bag, and that he never noticed.
He said 'I know son, around £5 each time. I never gave you much money when you were young. Your Mum didn't want me to spoil you.

But I felt you had earned the odd fiver'.

THE TROUBLED MAN

He got into the taxi and he was very drunk.

One way I deal with that is to hold them in conversation. It stops them falling asleep.

Somewhere in the journey he started to get agressive, and by then I had had enough.

I told him to button his lip or I would stop the car.

You would not talk to me like that if you knew what I have been through he said.

'We all have our problems,' I said,' and you are not the only problem I have, so be quiet'.

A couple of months later he was back in the car with 3 other guys, so I headed over to Dundrum, He was out of control again.We went to his house first and as he was getting out he nearly fell on his face. One of the guys from the back caught him and walked him to his house.

One of his other friends said "You would never guess what that guy went through in the last 10 years"

So the story was told;

When he was young his life was so different.

His family was extremely wealthy.

They had chefs, butlers, maids, gardeners, chauffeurs, and high status in society.

They had houses in California, Monaco, The Hamptons, Downtown New York. Each house had cars and staff at the ready. When they went to the airport they passed all the lines of people waiting. Their car drove up to their private jet and away they went.

Then one day everything changed. The father was arrested, put on trial and got natural life in jail. All the property was seized and sold to pay back the investors..

He had only a few dollars in his pocket. Everything was sold to repay his victims.

He was not guilty of any crime himself, but the sins of the father fall on the sons.

He suffered badly as a result. His entire lifestyle changed overnight. Everything he had taken for granted was gone, most of all the good name of his family

His father had been involved in the biggest corporate fraud up to the time of Enron.

A family friend brought him over to Ireland, he finished his education, met an Irish girl and got married.

He changed his family name to hers and began a new life in Ireland.

He is the cleverest trader in the bank and he makes them a lot of money.

But he had to lie about his name on his job application and he is in dread of the bank finding out about his true identity.

He is a haunted man.

THE VOICE

I forget where I picked this lady up. But she was going to Mount Argus and she was wearing sunglasses at night time.

We spoke briefly and then a cowboy song came on the radio. "Oh higher that up " she said in her Donegal accent. Then she sang in the most wonderful harmony I ever heard. The hair stood up on the back of my neck, it was really different.

When it was over I said you have the most wonderful voice I ever heard.

She said, why didn't you join in.

No I would have spoiled it all I said.

Then she told me that when I was driving around on my own I should sing out loud, it helps your breathing and lifts your spirit.

Listen here I said if you ever want to go professional we could make a lot of money together.

No I'm not that good at all.

So we reached journey's end and I thanked her again for the song.

She was paying me and she pushed the dark glasses back onto her head to see the money better.

I knew her straight away. But I couldn't put a name to

her. She said good night in Irish and was gone

A few days later I was taking luggage out of the car on Liffey St. when I saw her looking at me from the record shop.

Enya !

I thought her voice was all produced in a studio.
But my performance was really pitch perfect.

STUPID PADDY

I was at the Westbury hotel and there was a guy smoking outside.

How are you son? It's a grand day.

I agreed and the conversation opened up.

Paddy's the name.

They used to call me stupid Paddy.

But they don't call me that now

I'm from Cabra me but you wouldn't know that to hear me talking.

Me daddy took us to Yorkshire when I was 6.

My daddy had us kids working on the buildings from the time were 12 years old.

If he did that now he would be arrested.

But it did me no harm.

I was around 15 and I was putting flashing along the side of a roof.

The way it's done is, there a groove cutinto the concrete and you push the lead sheeting into the groove. Then you hammer in a plug of lead with a bolster. If the plug is the right size it grips the sheet of lead tight, if not, you have to go at it again.

Hit and miss.

Then one day I had an idea and I made a clip out of steel. After a few small changes I invented the Flashing clip.

Here it is Paul, giving me a packet of them.

We cannot keep up the supply of them.

You can do 10 yards of flashing in ½ an hour.

Nothing like it has come before.

I have a World patent.

Our biggest shop is Amazon .

Then a few years ago a mate came to me.

Paddy you are very handy with bending a bit of tin could you make me a bracket to hold a solar panel in place.

I need one for made for retro fitting,

He gave me a solar panel and I set to work. It was hard to do. I had to change the thickness of the metal bracket 4 times. Then one morning as I was making up the final change for the bracket an idea came to me. If the Flashing clip was a really big thing, this idea was a huge money spinner.

I had invented a bracket for holding a solar panel.

But I didn't do this just to make money.

I did it so my kids wouldn't have to struggle and so my grandchildren could get the best education going.

Just then a gleaming Rolls Royce came up from the car park below. ' Here comes my car now', he said.

I thought he was joking. No.

He opened the driver's door and got in.

It was one of those doors which opens from the front.He closed the door with the faintest click and let down the window.

By the way Paul, its a long time since they called me Stupid Paddy.

I waved at him as the car moved off without a sound.

ONE HAND WASHES THE OTHER

One day driving along the quays from Heuston station a guy walked across the road in front of us. My passenger said "Look at that man, he has one of the most successful legal practices in Ireland and it all came from a small favour he did for someone"

There was a girl working for one of the big German retail giants. She was a trainee manager. But her training involved endless filling of shelves and little else.

There were two other girls who worked with her on the shop floor, but they were always chatting and doing very little work.

She would separate them and instruct one to work here and the other to work on the opposite side of the shop. But within ten minutes they had stopped work and were back together talking.

They were awful chatterboxes and she went to the managers several times to get them to help her deal with it.

Nothing was ever done to resolve the problem.

Then one day after separating them three or four times in an hour she exploded and shouted at them.

The two girls went to management and said that they were being bullied and they were going to sue the store.

So the trainee manager was suspended and she was to be sacked subject to investigation.

Her dad was a taxi driver and a really good golfer and his partner was that same barrister. He told the barrister about the problem his daughter was having.

Tell her to write down everything that happened, right from the first day she started work. Every little thing, in chronological order and bring it to my office.

The barrister went through the list and they added a few things that she had missed out on.

Then she remembered that she had submitted three ideas which the company had adopted and she had never got paid for them. So they typed up the letter and found out who they should send the letter to in Germany and posted it off.

On the big day she was called into the store and the store managers were working on the shop floor. They turned their backs on her as she passed through to the office without a greeting, a bit strange, she thought.

There in the office she was met by three German guys who greeted her with warm handshakes and big smiles.

First of all we should not be here.
When we got your letter we came over early to resolve this problem.

This has come to pass because of laziness and dishonesty of the management team here.

The managers are working on the shop floor today, we will probably sack them all.

We will train you up to the standard that you are well capable of achieving and we are building a new store for you to manage in Co.Kildare.

Yes, said one of the other guys, and the ideas which you gave us?
Your managers stole those ideas and took the money for themselves.

That money will be in your bank account by the weekend.

We are looking for some way of stopping this ever happening again in the future.

After all if you give an idea and then someone else steals it you will not put forward any more ideas.

What about the two girls?

They have been sacked, we showed them video tapes of their work performance and one of them was also sacked for stealing.

So she went back to work, the management team were replaced and things went really well. One day two of the German managers came in smiling and told her that they were all going for a mystery day trip.

It was to Co.Kildare to the new store which was almost finished.

This is your baby now, good luck.

We know that it is safe in your hands.

So she moved to Kildare and the store opened with balloons and clowns.

A few weeks later a woman fell over a tin of peas and sued the store.

Our girl rang head office."No we don't have anyone who deals with that, you are the manager, you deal with it".

So she rang her barrister friend who was delighted that she was doing so well now.

He took on the case and won!
Now he does all the legal work for that supermarket chain in Ireland.

It just goes to show how one hand washes the other

LONG NIGHTS JOURNEY INTO DAY.

Back in the 80's, a friend of mine was driving a hackney cab and he pulled into the Centra in Rathmines to buy some cigarettes.

There were 2 two guys standing outside the shop,one of them carrying a bag.

They were looking for a taxi and he said that he would take them.

So they got in and they started giving him directions to drive all over the city.

As they went along they would stop to talk to groups of youths here and there.

Eventually they arrived out at the Nutgrove shopping centre which was under construction at the time. As usual one guy got out and the other guy sat in the back with the bag.

He was getting tired so he asked the guy on the back seat what they were up to?

He just opened up.
"We were in an open prison in England together and a friend of ours gave us a contract to whack a fella. We're looking for him, thats all"

Go on outa that! he said.

No, No Look and he opened the bag with £8,000 and a Glock pistol.

Hold on a minute he said, ' You do know that that's a Glock ?.

No its a gun.
Do you know nothing!

Thats a 9mm Glock pistol, it has a hell of a kick when you fire it.

'Do you know how to fire it? Do you not just pull the trigger?' asked the young man

No! You have to cock it.

This puts a bullet in the breach.
Then you have to make sure that the safety catch is off.

As I told you there is a mighty kick from that gun when she goes off, you might have to hold it with both hands.

The second guy arrived back and he went berserk.
"Why the hell did you go and tell him for?"

He just talked sense with him and calmed down the situation, He told them how they would spook the guy they were looking for going around like this and anyhow in all likelihood the gun would not fire for them when the time came if they didn't know how it worked.

Go up into the mountains and fire two shots tomorrow.

Don't forget to put the safety catch back on when you are finished.

So they gave up for the day and he drove them over to Tallaght where one of their grandmothers lived.

They paid him £50
'What would you have done if we decided to shoot you?,' the

leader of the two said to my friend.

He pulled out a teak baton from the side of the seat.

But we have a gun, the boss of the two said.
'But I know how to shoot your gun and you don't.'

They laughed and went off.

So he drove off and pulled over around 500 yards further on for a pee and promptly fell flat on his face shaking with shock.

When he had composed himself, he drove to a Garda Station with his story but was told not to be wasting their time.

The next day he spoke to a friend of his who was a Garda. Two days later he got a phone call from him. 'It's about them 2 fellas from the other night.

We caught them, with the gun and the bag of money.'

Thanks for that, that is worth 2 speeding tickets for you.
He rang him back later on to find out if the gun had been fired?

Yes they had fired 2 practice shots.

HEAVY BREATHING

A young girl of around 20 jumped into the taxi.
RTE was her destination, "Have you Asthma" I asked.

"No, I have CF! I wish it was just asthma."

She told me of her condition and how she will have to have a lung and heart transplant to live.

But today she was going on to a radio programme to kick up hell about something that had taken place in one of the local hospitals.

Her name was Orla Tinsley and she is a great person. I found her again on Facebook..

CF patients have very low immune systems and the CF organization had built a wing onto a hospital and kitted it out to isolate the patients. But now the hospital was using some of the beds for ordinary patients.

This means that none of that entire wing can be used for the treatment of the CF patients.

We had arrived and she was going to give them hell on the airwaves.

I said that I loved the way that she never complained about her own condition and I would like to do something small to help her if she would not be offended.

The taxi-ride is on the house with my blessing and I would love to give you a big hug. But I wouldn't like to kill you",

"I could think of worse ways of going" she said with a big laugh and she was gone,

I often thought of her through the years, and then one day she was on the radio from her hospital bed in New York recovering from her heart/lung transplant,

She had paid for her operation through crowd funding.

It seems that the internet saved her life.
People like her have a special place in my mind and in my heart.

You would love to have her for a daughter.

ARNOLD CLARKE

He hopped in at the Marker hotel and introduced himself.

He looked at my ID and he said with a big laugh "Bloody hell Paul when are you going to retire?

Only kidding son! I am 84 and I still go to work every day.

I go into the office and say do this, do that and even throw papers around.

Then I go home and watch Judge Judy. Its the work that keeps you young,

I am over here because I have been awarded best car dealer in Europe and best after sales service,"

I shook his hand, not knowing whether to believe him. His two sons and daughter in law were coming.

They got in and we talked among ourselves about cars until we reached Wicklow St close to Grafton St. I had to get out to open the back door for the daughter in law.

She said "Come on Dad we'll buy you a new coat"

He said "I don't need a new coat I have two coats at home"

"But Dad, you didn't bring a coat and its very very cold".

'Look over there', I said. 'That's Louis Copeland's shop, he will look after you. Arnold Clarke had walked around to my side of the car and he put €20 into my hand.

"No its only €10 "I said and he said "Paul its 10 for the fair and 10 for the tip"

I don't know why I looked him up in Wikipedia but I did.
Arnold Clarke, Born in Glasgow in an area called the Townhead, a tough poor area of Glasgow.

Aged 14 he left school and started to make his way in the world, when the second world broke out he got a job in the Royal Air Force as a mechanic.

When he left the RAF he was in charge of training the mechanics.

He got £70 demob money when he left and with that money he bought an old car and did it up and sold it. And then went into the motor trade.

He opened his first garage in Parkhead in 1954 and he expanded to become the biggest independent car dealer in Europe.

When I met him his turnover was £2 billion.

I would love to meet him again as he was a very interesting man to talk to.

He knew his cars as well.
 He did a clever thing to facilitate his customers and thereby to promote sales. A would-be customer would see a car, then go off to organise a loan.But many of them did not come back, so he opened his own bank in every one of his garages. He also PCP to the UK.
There was so much I would have liked to have asked him, I wrote to the main garage in Glasgow but got no reply. But it is a very big operation.   A short time later on I found that he had died.

I would have loved to have brought him to a certain garage here in Dublin

Just to look at it and see for himself.

One of the taxi drivers here had cash, his parents had passed away and they sold the family home and divided the money and he wanted to buy a Mercedes car, so with his cash in his pocket and he walked into the showroom.

The salesman stopped him at the door by putting his hand on his chest, caught him by the arm turned him around and marched him back out through the front door.

"We don't want any of you time wasters coming in here. You can afford nothing in this showroom so get out, and don't be wasting our time."

He went to another garage and his money was very welcome.

Just because a person dresses in a certain way doesn't mean that they have money or not.

I was in London with my son around Park Lane and saw an Audi r8 through the window in a car showroom.

The salesman came outside to us and brought us in and he showed us the car in great detail. Also there was another make of car called Skyline I think (It is the Lexus of the Datsun line).

God this is really great I said, I really enjoyed it, but we have no money.

That doesn't matter, when you have some money or you know someone else who has some money send them in to me.

Then he noticed that some real customers had come in.

His plan was simple. If anyone saw someone in the showroom it would bring other people in.

DEATH BY A THOUSAND KNIFE CUTS.

It really is that way now.

You have to get yourself vetted by the police have this paper stating you have tax clearance certificates, your car has to be certified in a testing facility and the list goes on.

The Garda allow rickshaws to operate without any paperwork or insurance at all.

At venues like the 3 Arena they forbid taxis to get near to it and allow the rickshaws free access. This is the way that death by 1,000 knife cuts works.

So I brought my car in to be tested for the NCT and they said that the right headlight was out of alignment and I went to the garage, he said it was only very slightly out and he adjusted it,.When I went back I was told that the left headlight was out.

I asked why it had passed before and now it had failed. "Just get it fixed"

John in the garage said that it was perfect and he told me just to bring it back again and another guy tested it. I got the cert and renewed the licence.

I still felt a bit sore so I sent in a letter of complaint.

A week later I got a phone call from the NCT in Ballymun.

"We read your letter and we have decided that you adjusted it yourself."

There has to be a stick to keep organisations like them in line.

A neighbour of mine who is a mechanic worked on the big aeroplane engines at the airport
He brought his mother's car up for a test. As he had the testing kit in the aircraft hanger he tested the emissions. They were fine and he headed to the test centre.

He waited and the tester came out. "It's failed on the emissions"

Look, I tested this at the airport an hour ago and it passed, could you check it on another machine? "NO"

So my neighbour knew someone and rang a supervisor in the NSAI (They set standards and procedures) He explained his problem and the supervisor asked for the technician to be brought to the phone.

He put the gun to his head and he told him.
"If you refuse to check this car on a different machine now we will come over and close you down for 3 days while we check every screwdriver and piece of paperwork in the facility."

He ran it through on a different machine and it passed.

They were then told to bring back everyone that had been failed on that machine and to re-test them for nothing.

That evening the NSAI arrived over to the test centre and reviewed the video tapes which showed that the machines had not been calibrated for weeks.

(It's simple, you just test one against the other)
They were fined but I know now they are back at their old tricks again.

You need standards, but standards have to be seen to be fair, and there has to be someone looking over everyone's shoulder.

This goes for the Police and the politicians as well.

I have just written to the EU commission about the car testing organization being a monopoly and as such it is totally against EU rules.

It should be a franchise given to independent garages under a supervisory organization. Like in the UK, Holland, France etc

THE WAVING CAT.

I was finished for the day when I picked up this chap in Clontarf going to a phone shop in Mary St, he wanted me to wait for him until he got a quick phone fix.

I was there only one minute when a woman Garda came over.

"Get a move on now or you'll get a ticket."

So I drove forward and there right outside the toy shop was a stranded family.

"Please help us we spent too long with Santa and now we might miss our train home.

The husband was dying of cancer; his hair was all gone from the radiation treatment, a young enough guy. They had 2 small kids; his poor wife was really suffering.

As we headed for Heuston station the little girl put her hand down the side of the seat and found a wallet full of money.

The wallet had fallen down through the space at the corner of the back seat. Her dad was delighted with her. "Orla you are such a lucky girl, you found somebody's wallet and Paul will make sure that the man gets it back, he will be so happy"

After I dropped them at the station I went home. Traffic was very heavy as it was close to Christmas Eve.

When I got home I opened the wallet and there was a

big bundle of notes,
Irish Pound notes and Sterling.

In total £1,600 His driving licence and blood donor cards etc.

No Facebook back then.

So I rang directory enquiries and I got his number.

When I rang the number I spoke to the person in the UK. At first he said "No he is not here any longer" As soon as I said I was ringing from Dublin "OH you have found my wallet.

Could you post it back to me please?"

There was a bit of discussion I said that there was too much money to be sending in the post. He told me to open out the wallet and wrap it in cardboard.

Put it into a good strong envelope and send it by registered post as a book of no commercial value. I did so putting in my name and address and phone number.

So I took £10 out of the wallet to cover postage and went to the post office. It cost me £13.60.

Still its only £3.60 lost, So off it went. I heard nothing for 4 days and I went back to the post office, "Yes that parcel was delivered the next day"
I had lost his contact details.

To this present time I never got a simple call to say thank you.

A friend of mine said that I should have taken out the money and posted back the empty wallet.

Still that was not me. But a small thank you would have been something.

I told the story many times and then I had some people
from India in the car.

My friend I am much older than
you are and I tell you this,
Some people do not believe in any God,
Others do not believe in Karma

Strange to say others do not
believe in the life hereafter.

Some people do not believe
in heaven or hell.
Some do not even believe
in reincarnation.
But I am telling you this.

Some day you will be walking down
the street minding your own business
when something catches your eye.
It will be a waving cat from the
window of a Chinese shop.

You buy it and bring it home.

This is that same thoughtless
man now living in his next life.

Fecking useless in his past life

and Fecking useless in
the next life too.

So he now sits in the bay window of
my house waving at the postman.

He must be wondering why he
was so stupid in his last life.

THE INCREDIBLE STORY

Would you take American Dollars? 25/5/2006

So there I was at the airport and I was number 10 or 12 in Queue.

I could see a guy walking along the rank asking each driver in turn saying. No, No,No.

Whatever he was selling he was not having much luck.
Then he came to me.
"Would you accept American dollars?"

The answer Yes brought a smile to his face.
"Follow me back to the front door and I will get the rest of my party".

He came out with a teenage boy and girl and a woman in tow. The woman did not speak even when I spoke to her. So I reckoned she was not his wife. I loaded up the luggage.

All great journeys begin with the words.

"Where are we going?"

The K club was his reply.

I'll get the sheet.

Why? Is there something wrong?

No! It is outside the city limits so I have to show you the cost from the beginning.

Its €80.

 Ok! thats $100. Into my hand he counted the money into my hand 20,40,60,80,100.

Ok folks! buckle up.

After a while I noticed that he was playing with a game boy. Here I'll turn on the light. Are you playing football? Is that a Game Boy??

No its a Blackberrry. I am sending an email (Whatever that was back then)

He told me that this phone would send and receive emails and texts, it had a diary, a phone book, a camera and an alarm clock.

Throw it away it will drive you mad.

No No you don't understand. It is brilliant.

I will just finish this and then we can talk.

5 Minutes later he said "Im finished"

As I put up my hand to turn off the light I saw him clearly for the first time.

Hey! I know you ?..

No, I am nobody famous.

No I didn't think you were famous

But I have met you before.

Honestly if I had met you I would remember you he said.

Did you ever work in an electrical wholesalers in Bray?

No I have always worked for myself and the conversation went back to normal.

Where are you from? Los Angeles California,
I would love to go there to visit the Magic Castle.

I know it, its on Franklin Ave.
Yes thats right.

Have you ever been there?

No. But I really want to go there sometime. The kids behind said Dad when you go will you bring us too? When can we go?

So he said we will go there on the Thursday after we get home.

Hold on a minute I said. You can't just turn up. You have to know someone to vouch for you to get you in.

It's a private members club.
I think I know someone who will get me in.

So we talked a little about magic.

Then I mentioned that there was a great book about Hollywood called "The moon's a balloon"
by David Niven.

I have that book, is it not called "Bring on the empty horses?"

He was right as well, there are 2 books

He seemed to know most of the places and a lot of the people in the book, but why not, he lived there.

I was telling him that I looked on actors with a Jaundiced eye as I had worked with a casting director for a few weeks called John Hubbard.

We would go to the actors houses ring the doorbell and bang the door until we got a response.

The actors were all instantly recognisable when they came to the door. "What the hell are you banging on my bloody door for at this hour of the morning?"

"Hubbard casting" I would say and it was like hitting a light switch.

Oh Hello John.   Great to see you.

We would get them to sign for the manuscript and then we were off to disturb the next sleepyhead.

In my mind I could never reconcile why these actors did not have part time jobs, John told me at the time that when an actor is not working he is resting.

But why do you have no time for them? said my passenger

Look! Acting is a wonderful craft.

I have seen many wonderful productions of Arthur Miller plays that bring you to a different world.

But I find that acting is so superficial. It is such a cutthroat world. they are all after the limelight and the big roles.

I don't see how a wholesome family life could fit with all that.

No No Paul, I can assure you that most actors are faithful family people.

Then he said

Do you like Movies?.

Of course, Have you seen anything lately?

Well I saw two movies of similar ilk. "No country for old men" and a drugs movie called "Traffic".

Tell me about them.

So the next 20 minutes were spent talking about the movies.

Then he said. You have a great eye I didn't notice that mistake you told me about in the Traffic movie but I have the director's cut I will get the copy that was released and check it out,one against the other, to see for myself.

But whats your favourite movie of all time?

Cinema Paradiso, without a doubt I said.

It is set in Sicily, the casting of actors is perfect.

How they found that young boy ToTo and how they controlled him is beyond me. I have seen the movie many times and there is something different to see in it each time.

Like what?

The way the square changes through the movie.

The cars and the peoples' clothes.

That wind that comes from Africa in the autumn.

The swallows screaming as they fly past.

The local scenery creates a wonderful set for the movie.

Then there is one wonderful thing in that movie and

that is the music of Morricone. I don't know if you understand how the music can make or break a movie.

Oh I do know that for sure! He said.

I just let you talk on there for a bit.
That movie is my favourite one by far as well.

He asked me if I had ever considered working on movies.

No its not me. Sitting around for hour after hour, knowing that the lens is wrong for that shot and not being able to tell the director.

Then after 2 days your work finds its way to the cutting room floor.

No it's not really like that.
Movie making is cooperation between a group of professional people,the director,camera

man and the script writer have to listen to each other and the best job gets done.

When you create that special scene and the people jump up and applaud there is no better feeling.

I still had no idea who he was.

'Hey heres one for you,' I said. The architect who did the refurbishment on the K club has a car that once belonged to Prince Charles.

What make is it?
Aston Martin.

Green? Yes

I have been in it.

That is one awful colour.

No its historical.

British racing green.

I have an Aston Martin myself.

I asked what she was like to go?

No you can't speed where I live you can only drive at 30 mph if you can even get up to that.

Perhaps I was tired but I didn't pick up on that either.

I told him that I was going to England to Donnington Park race track to drive a Ferrari on a racing track for my 60th birthday. He thought that would be a great idea.(It was too, I reached 180 MPH)

So we drove into the K club and he asked me if I would come back that evening and bring him to Dublin and drop him back down again.

Well no,I said.They have a beautiful limo here and they will drive you up and down in style, at no cost.

No I want to go in your van.

Look, it is 4 journeys for me and I would only be paid for 2.

If you measure just one leg of the trip , I will pay 5 times that amount he said...

There is a bigger problem. Its my wife's birthday and she would kill us all.

Sometimes she says that she would divorce me if she could remember for sure what I looked like.

Oh no don't worry Paul, I have enjoyed this trip so much.

Thank you.

So we shook hands and went our separate ways.

That night on the Late Late show

Mr. Nobody- famous was introduced.

And he said

Before I start Pat I have to say hi to someone .

"Hello Paul, I hope you're watching.

Thanks for looking after us this morning,

I enjoyed it so much and I am really looking forward to meeting you again".

Isn't that nice of Steven Speilberg to say thanks

That was on 25th May 2006.

About the $100?

I went to a magic convention in England shortly afterwards..

One of the American magicians had a baby daughter who was born with a hole in her heart.

Imagine that, a poor sick baby?

In The Land Of The Free if you have no health insurance or money you will die.

So I put the money into an envelope and wrote on the outside.

"This money came from the hand of Steven Spielberg; I hope it will help your daughter"

The following year I met that magician in Blackpool, I

asked him how his daughter was?

"Oh gee Paul, she is getting on fine now"

Then I told him that I was the person who gave him the $100 from Steven Spielbergs hand.

"Oh my God! How wonderful!. I put it into a safety deposit box and I will give it to her when she is 18 !"

John Hubbard made a movie with Steven later on called Lincon.

I hope they enjoyed each other's company.

I told this story to a German girl once and she totally dismissed me.

"Do you think I am Stupid !

Steven Spielberg he would have helicopter to bring him to the K club."

'You are right.

If he didn't need to collect stories, that would have been the way to go'.

This is the one story Spielberg really loved.

Just after I had started telling it, he began to write it down.

When I finished he said If I ever lived to be a hundred I don't think I would ever have imagined such a frightening tale.

He told me that he has a notebook beside his bed with a pen and pencil at all times and a notebook in his pocket..

A thorough man.

All the stories and thoughts are written into two sets of diaries, one set is kept in a safe in his office, the other set is in a safe in his home. The diaries go back more than 50 years.

A fire will not put him out of business.

He really jumped when I said "Stick it on a computer"

These thoughts are my life's work, I couldn't allow anyone to get at them.

The story was the following;

The drug addict

One day in bad light a guy jumped into the front seat of my taxi. I would not have stopped for him if I had seen him first.

I turned to ask him where he was going and I saw his face and looked into those haunted eyes.

OH hell! I gasped!

What are you looking at me like that for?
I was once a normal person like you!

Crumlin ! he said.

I had a business, a house,a beautiful wife and kids.

But there was something missing somewhere deep in my soul, I didn't really know what it was.

I was at a party one night and a friend gave me a shot of Heroin.

God! the peace and the feeling of drifting just off the ground came over me.

Were you ever in Love?
Course you were.

She was a beautiful blonde and she looked at me.

I looked into her wonderful blue eyes and I was lost.

I knew from that moment that we were to be together for all time. When she touched me it was like a feather stroking my skin.

The smell of her perfume moved me to heaven.
We danced and made love,we laughed and then we fell asleep together, her gentle breathing on my skin was bliss.

Then I needed her and sometimes I couldn't find her. I had to rob and steal to get money.

One morning,I felt her move beside me I could
get this awful stench and there she was.

No longer beautiful, her teeth were black, her skin, paper thin and covered in bruises and sores, her eyes sunken and bloodshot.

Hello you sicko! She said.

Don't try to run away from me,
I am inside you now.
FOREVER
You can't get rid of me now, even if you try.

I have managed to give up the drugs, but my body will
never heal.

My business and family are long gone, I hurt a lot of
people on that journey.

I hurt myself most of all.

I work with drug addicts now and they trust me because I, like them, have been through hell.

THE ANGEL

Heuston station is a good taxi rank, well 15 years ago it was much better.

Too many taxis now, where there was 6 cars back then there are 50 now.

So there I was listening to the radio when a man I didn't see approached me.

Hello mate ! How much to Maynooth university? I've missed the bloody train.

I think it was around €40, he hesitated, then I said that you know that I have to come back empty?

Yea all right mate!

Look I will leave the meter on so that you can see you are not being robbed.

So we set off for Maynooth, me and my new Australian friend.

Aussies are good talkers and I will not tell you what his subject was in case I identify him, it was a very unusual subject for sure.

Is there much of a drugs problem here in Dublin?

In Melbourne it has really taken off.

Crack cocaine, its everywhere. It's easier to get your hands on than a bag of sugar.

We had a daughter who was wild. She would go missing for 2 or 3 days at a time.

Each time she went missing she would come home exhausted and sleep and eat.

We talked to her, tried to get her to come around, we even paid for help.

Then when she was 15 she disappeared for 4 weeks. We went to the police.

We stormed heaven with prayers and I spent time going around looking for her.

The police said that they would keep a lookout for her and time went on.

Four weeks from the time that she went missing she was found in a very bad way, she was dehydrated and starving.

Worst of all were the track marks on her arms. She had been given Heroin and was used as a sex slave during her incarceration.

The time in hospital was a time for great tears.

Tests were made, at least she did not have AIDS

or VD but she was pregnant.

My wife is a staunch Catholic and she was adamant that there would be no abortion.

A little girl was born. We called her Mary, though everyone that knows her calls her Angel.

I know I am her grandfather, but what a super wonderful child she is.

She is beautiful and has the wonderful blue eyes like her mother had.

She dances around the garden singing to the birds in the morning, she laughs all the time and she is the centre of our entire world.

Her mother went away when Angel was 3 months old and she was found dead in a derelict house 6 months later.

Another chapter closed in my life.

But that little Angel keeps us all going.

This new drug Crack Cocaine is so addictive. Crime is way way up all over the World.

I do believe that a drug will come very soon that will sweep through entire cities taking every adult with it. Behind there will be thousands of orphans crying.

I have seen mothers singing in the church choir and a week later they are selling sex on the street corner, because the drug problem is so acute and the numbers of women available on the streets have grown so much so the price of sex has dropped a lot.

Angel started school just before I came over here, the same thing happened as happened when she went to play school. All the kids rushed over and hugged her, the teacher got emotional as she had never seen such a spontaneous moment of pure love for anyone.

You know I never knew that something so wonderful could come from something so evil.

But it did. It is like God put out his hand to stop the tragedy and created a miracle.

Life is good and bad

You just do your best

Then he was gone.

There are many lessons to be learned when you drive a taxi

CLOSE OF BUSINESS.

I was still working for Metro when a call came in to go to Ringsend for a job.

It was to a betting shop which is right on the bend there.

I waited and a gentleman came out and he was off to the airport.

There was no Sam Beckett Bridge or port tunnel back then so progress was slow.

I was working on a card trick called B'wave by Phil Goldstein.

It involved 4 cards, you count them face down using the Elmlsey count.

I was doing it every time the car stopped.

What are you doing? He said. So I told him that it was a

little card trick.

Will you do it for me?

No I would have to do it a few hundred times more to get it right.

He said that he wouldn't judge me, but he would love to see how it worked out.

OK I have 4 queens showing the backs, 1,2,3 and 4 (Elmsley count, one card is counted twice)

Red or black (Magicians choice) Red he said so I reject the 2 black cards.

Queen of Hearts or Queen of Diamonds ?

Hearts he said.

Do you want to change your mind? 5,4,3,2,1

You are happy with Hearts?

Then I fanned out the two cards in my hand and the Queen of hearts had turned face up.

I put the unturned card with the other 3 cards.

Then I turned over the card and the back was a blue backed card while the others were all red backed.

I knew that you would choose that one. Turn the other 3 cards over .

The other cards had no faces, ie blank cards

He was gobsmacked!

He was from Bristol and I told him that there was a magic shop in The Crescent in Bristol

I told him to go there between Tuesday and Thursday around 11 am when they would not be busy and they would coach him on how to do it.

 He had just sold his bookmaker business and Ladbrooks are in there now.

He thought that there was no future for betting shops in Ireland.

At the airport he gave me £20 and told me to keep the change.

Then he said, Paul would you take Sterling?

I said sure and he gave me another £60!

Whats this for?

Thats for showing me that wonderful trick.

It was really great.

Tipping is a thing that working class people do, because they know the value of money.

That is still the biggest tip I ever got to this day.

The pity of the internet is that everyone will Google that trick and know how it's done.

As Paul Daniels said ' Magic is the best fun you can have with your clothes on'

THE SOLDIER FROM JAPAN

I have a good few talents thank God, one of them is security.

Working with locks and making things safe is easy for me to do.

So I was asked to come and have a look at a car in a garage located in Sutton.

He had a nice car locked in a garage and the door was not very secure.

I got a big bracket type lock which fitted to the door and the other end on to the ground.

So a price was agreed and I returned the next morning with my tools. I had to bring 2 extension cables to bring power to the garage.

He was a tall Londoner, retired and I asked him what he had worked at.

He asked me to guess and he laughed at my efforts.

When I gave up he told me that he was the biggest silk trader in the UK!

There was quite a story in that for sure.

When he was younger he was in the army fighting against the Japanese and he got captured. They were very badly treated and they would have all been killed had they not started a building project for the Japanese.

Did you ever hear of "The Bridge over the river Quai?

That was it!, We were building them a bridge and because of that we were kept alive.

We were nearly at deaths door when we were liberated, I am 6ft 2 and on liberation I weighed 4 stone. After liberation a lot of guys died. They were living for that moment freedom came and when it came they could not go on.

When I got stronger I had some really bad news.

My entire family had been wiped out in the blitz in London.

I mourned for 10 days and then I realized that that I had to put all that in the past and move on with my life.

We got our demob money, not a fortune, but the first money I had seen in ages.

I asked for permission to go to China and a group of us went over.

I loved the place, so different to what I was ever used to.

I found a guide and he brought me around and we we went to a cloth market and there I found guys selling the most beautiful silk you ever saw.

I spent all my demob money and I bought as much silk as I could carry.

I also took the stallholders names and addresses.

When we came back to London I took a bolt of silk and brought it to a dressmaker.

She cried and cried. She had not seen silk for nearly 6 years.

It was like a bar of solid gold. I sold it in sections and sent an order to my friends back in China for more.

Soon we had a turnover of more than £10,000 per week.

I liked it, I loved the Chinese people and we still have a house over there.

He was a very modest man, very cultured and a real pleasure to meet.

So once more there is a moral.

There is good around you if you look for.

Do not let the bad things blind you.

LOOSE ENDS

So as I wind down

I want to pass on some simple tips that might well save you the price of this book or more.

Driving

Always have your car seat forward. So far forwards that if you have to brake hard in an emergency that your leg will still be bent, if your leg is straight on impact in a crash the femur will be shot through your hip, if your leg is bent your knee will flex.

Dishwashers,

Never let them run and then go out or go to bed.

They are a big source of domestic fires.

Tumble dryers with blocked filters are also high on the danger list.

Keys, Keys, Keys

If I could find the man who invented them I would lock him up and throw away the key.!!!

Not quite that bad.

When you buy a new house change the locks front and back, you don't know who has a spare Key

Car keys, always have a spare car key, buy a battery for the key now, get it with the same model number, those numbers mean something.

If your car only came with one key get another made. Use a locksmith, not a garage.

The new key is made by cloning the existing key. If you lost the only key you have then the car has to be re-keyed and that can cost€1500 at least.

Here is something else.

Smart keys

You walk up to the car, the key is in your pocket you just touch the door handle and the car unlocks, you get in keys still in your pocket and drive away.Now when you get out you touch the 2 little lines on the door handle and the car locks itself.

Thieves can pick up your signal and away they go in your wonderful hi tec car.

A driver from the UN showed me how easy it is to do simply, using a mobile phone.

You can buy a RF blocking pouch and all our own cars have a steering wheel "Crooklock"

Right back to the 60s with that one.

Also the keys are all kept in a tin box on the hall table.

One last thing, If the keys have gone behind your mobile phone in your pocket the car will not get a signal.

If you have a Porsche and it is a hot summers day you might be tempted to take off your jacket and throw it into the boot. When you close the boot the car locks itself.

 Stupid boy, the keys are in the jacket pocket and you are locked out.

This one is wild!

Ring your house, "Sorry to bother you, get my spare car key from the drawer in my desk and I will ring you back on your mobile."

When you ring again you say. Hold the key up to the phone and count to 5 and then press unlock button on the key.

You put your phone on speaker, hold it up to the car lock and do you know what?

Nine times out of ten the car itself

Laptops.

Never leave a laptop on a bed or a soft surface, the ducts where the cooling air circulates will be blocked and you will have a fire.

Never ever buy a wristwatch from a man who is out of breath.

It will be stolen !

THE ANGELS
OF MERCY.

So I picked up 6 wonderful angels of mercy (Nurses) from the Philippeans and they were going to the immigration office on Burgh quay.

They were working in Tralee general hospital, they even had Kerry accents and had to come to Dublin to renew their visas. They were truly wonderful girls.

They had jumped on the train at 7am When they would arrive in Dublin a friend of theirs would have pulled 6 tickets for the queue so that they would not have to wait long.

"This whole exercise is pointless, we have to come to Dublin from Tralee, get a form stamped and pay €50, just to carry on working."

The cost of all this would feed our families for 2 months back at home.

Not long afterwards the Australian government had a

shortage of nurses.

They offered them.

5 year working visa for them and their spouse.

Free healthcare,

Subsidised accommodation and free education for their children.

Guess What?

They all went to OZ ! They were closer to home as well.

Here is a simple example of the humanity of a Phillipina nurse.

It was a nursing home out near the airport.

I had a wheelchair taxi and I brought a man out for a week to give his wife and kids a break. As we were being checked in a woman came walking down the corridor crying. Big tears were streaming down her cheeks.

"Where am I? I'm lost, Where am I? Help me.

An Irish nurse was walking towards her, and she walked straight past her. Not even a glance. Then a Philipena nurse came out of an office pushing a wheelchair with a lady on it. She stopped and went to the distressed lady and put her arms around her. Mary, Mary, don't cry.

You know me don't you?

I am bringing Phyllis to her bedroom, come with us and we will put her into bed. Then I will bring you down to the cafe for a cup of tea and a chat.

Would you like that?

Such a warm caring person, good looking too!

THE IRISH EMIGRANT.

I dropped off in Jamess st. Hospital where a very attentive foreign nurse took my passenger in, even though she was just going off duty.

Coming back on the main road a really chatty Dublin woman jumped in.

I told her about the foreign nurse who had brought in my patient and how wonderful she was.

That was us in the 40s,50s,and 60s, we all had to pack our bags and go, there was nothing here for us. I went to London when I was 14, there was 12 kids in our house so I had to go, and as each one grew up we followed each other over to England.

I went with my best friend Kitty. We got jobs as auxiliary nurses in a hospital and we slept in a nurses home which was a mile away. The Kitty would sleep on in the morning and I had to shake her to get a move on, we were always late.

After a while we were called into the matrons office and given one last chance.

"If you are late once more you will be sacked"

The matron then called me aside and told me that I should just get up and come into work alone.

The next day we arrived in 20 minutes late and were sacked, by noon we were out on the street.

That evening they were unemployed and homeless.

We went into a McDonalds around 4pm and suddenly it really hit us.

We had no job and nowhere to sleep that night.

There was an Irish girl working there, she came from Mayo, Theresa was her name.

She talked to us between serving customers.

I get off at 6, there is a hotel just down the road, my cousin works there I will try and ring her to tell her that we are coming.

So by 7 we had new jobs as chambermaids. The next

morning we got uniforms,

Sunday we got the day off and on Monday morning Kitty would not get up for work again.

So I called her, got dressed and I went to work alone.

Kitty got sacked and she had to go back home to Dublin.

I was very lonely on my own but I had to get on with my life.

Around 5 years later I was up on the 6th floor of the hotel when I was about to get into the lift I saw my supervisor going to the lift as well. I said "HOLD IT" and that is the last thing I remember until I woke up in hospital.

The lift had collapsed down 6 floors into the basement.

She went through long a list of her broken bones.

I was in an induced coma for a long time, I should have been dead; but for the great doctors in London.

They patched me up and shipped me home to the rehabilitation hospital here in Dublin.

At first I stood, and then I took in the fresh air and rested.

Later I tried those parallel bars, to take a step, then another.

The pain was something else, but I kept at it. Then I graduated to crutches.

Then Christmas came and went and I was on 2 walking sticks 20 /30 steps a day.

Then I was on one stick. Oe of the doctors had once said said to me you will be in a wheelchair for the rest of your life.

I resented that.

Another few months later I was walking, carrying the stick, but not needing it. When I saw that Dr.Tom walk past me and I let fly with the stick and nearly cracked his stupid skull open.

Now who will always be in a wheelchair?

I shouted at him.

I have never even used a stick since.

I said that this cold day must be very hard on her as the metal rods down her spine would draw in the cold.

"Listen son, when I die and they cremate me they will have enough metal in me ashes to make a bicycle."

The Dublin people of the 50s and 60s were tough hard working people, just like the Polish and Latvians that are here today.

She was tougher than a diamond.

"In Dublin's fair city, where the girls are so pretty I first set my eyes on sweet Molly Malone"

KARMA

So on a Sunday morning I was outside the Conrad Hil-
ton hotel which is opposite the concert hall.
A nice sunny morning and the radio was on.
The concierge came out and blew his whistle, so I
drove forward. But before I could get out of thre car the
Concierge had thrown the suitcase into the boot and
slammed the door.
The woman shouted "Airport"
They were having an argument, it was like 2 dogs
worrying each other over a bone.
So to clear the air I told them to watch out for the movie
bing made on Fitzwilliam square.
"Driver do you think we are bloody stupid?
You are going round in circrles, just take us straight to
the airport now"
The only other way of getting here is to go down 2 one
way streets.I continued in silence.
So we arrived at the airport and I had his change ready.
"I hope you left enough time for your flight"
I said
"Corse we ave ya feckin moron" He said.
"Well the change of the hour has fucked up my day" I
said.
"Wat de ell are ya takin abat?" He said.

"The clocks ! They went forward an hour last night"

It took around 4 seconds for him to realise that he was the moron and he had missed his flight.

With smart phones this is unlikely to happen now.
But Karma gave me a wonderful surprise on that day.

CHRISTMAS WAS COMING

I got a call on the radio to go to the Saudi Embassy in Fitzwilliam St.

Then the sky exploded and a months rain fell in 20 minutes, I carried on regardless and arrived in ½ an hour from when I first got the call.

This lunatic came out cursing and shouting.

Why have you kept me waiting for half hour?

There was no way to make him happy.

Then he started to curse at me (As only an Arab can)

I told him to get out.

You have to bring me.

No! I do not have to do anything for you and if you

don't get out I will call the Garda.

That will be no good, I have diplomatic immunity.

(Just a point here, the staff do not have diplomatic immunity, only the ambassador}

I was putting my hand on the baton when something came to me out of the blue.

Think of your mother ! how will she feel to see you abuse people like this?

God, it was like hitting a light switch. He really cried and said how sorry he was. He was under pressure and begged for forgiveness.

So we started the journey and then I said that you lads will be at a loose end over the Christmas.

I have a good idea for you.

The Leopardstown race track has a Christmas race meeting.

You should book a box for the duration of the races.

Bring guests to the races and have a Saudi chef to prepare food.

All you guys love horses.

So he was totally elated and asked for my phone number (I gave him yours)

 Couple of years later I had a guy going to the embassy and I told him that story.

Paul I am very displeased that this has happened. I am the charge d'affaires of the embassy.

Please come inside and put your finger on his photograph and he will be on the flight back home to Saudi tonight.

No, that will not happen.

He was upset for sure, but I was able for him and he learned a lesson.

He will never do that again.

You are a really good man, most people would see this as an opportunity to crush their enemy, but you forgave him.

But I d**o know** who he is!

The Christmas race meeting is the best thing for us in our whole year.

Thank you so much for giving us that.

To have such a position he had to be of the royal family, of which there are many.

And then he was gone

THE JAPANESE POP STAR

Once I got a call from an old mate who asked me if I would like to do a few days work with him. It was to drive a film crew around. Two 8 seater VW mini buses and a Mercedes car, just 3 or 4 days work.

So we had the camera man, the sound man, electrician and all their gear, the stars went in the merc.

The crew was completed by the singer, his manager, a director and a Dutch girl who was the interpreter. The first 2 days were in Dublin and on the third day we went to Tara to the show jumping stables of Paul Darragh, I remember it was a wet enough morning and all the workers were sheltering in my bus talking.

The Japanese director could not make up his mind where to put the cameras, after the second moving the camera man gave the Japanese director a tripod and told him to move it where he wanted it. When he had decided where it was to be he would come back and put the camera on the tripod, but for one time only.

He would not move it again.

I don't know if you ever heard that Japanese people do not like to be corrected or lose face.

There was a big sulk!

I got out of the minibus for fresh air while this was going on.

A girl rode her horse up and greeted the singer and rode her horse around for a few minutes or so. She was really good looking and when she caught my eye I smiled, then she smiled and came over to me. "Do you know what the delay is?"

I told her that I thought that they really don't know what they were doing at all.

She jumped down off the horse and loosened her chin strap.

I had a magic trick which I was working on.

Here is a great magic trick where you take a €5 note and at your fingertips you fold it and fold it again. Then you blow on the banknote and it has turned into a €50.

I showed it to her and she laughed.I see that you like horses she said. Yes I used to work in a racing stable when I was younger.

Then she said."Please go over and tell them that seeing as I am doing this as a favour, I will only wait 10 minutes more" So I went over to the Dutch girl who shooed me away, I still told her even though she had turned away from me.

So I went back to the girl and I told her that she had really fantastic teeth, she laughed and told me that I really knew how to impress the ladies.

A few more minutes passed and she said.

"OK I am off. Would you be happy to take the horse back to the stable for me and tell them I'm gone."

I went over to the Dutch girl and she scowled at me." What do you want now?"

Nothing!, I am bringing the horse back to the stable. The girl is gone.

"What?" I told you before that she would go if you didn't start filming in 10 minutes. She is gone.

So frantic phone calls were made and she came back

again smi;ing.

She had a big smile when I helped her back on to the saddle and in 20 minutes the scene was shot.

The girl came back over to me then and jumped off the horse.

"Thank you so much for talking to me. I have to be so careful who I talk to. But it was really wonderful meeting you. Please ride my horse around for 10 or 15 minutes and then when he has warmed up pop him over a few jumps and then bring him back to the stables for me."

I said good bye.

When I brought the horse back to the stable a girl with her arm in a sling came over to show me where to put the tack.

My God! the Princess must really like you, she said.

Is that her name? Princess.

Did no one tell you who were talking to?

That was the King of Jordan's daughter. No one has ever been allowed to ride any of her horses. You are the first ever.

I saw the monogram on the saddle then.

'She was a really nice person' I said.

THE INVENTOR

He came from between Carrickmacross and Shercock and I am afraid I don't know his name.

He was a farmer and he had a very lively mind.

Once he bought a traction engine and when the harvest was over he stripped it all to the smallest pieces and displayed its works on the floor of his barn. People came from miles around and said that he would never be able to put it back together again. Not only did he put it back together but he modified the manifold and increased the horsepower.

He built a wind turbine and electrified the house and yard. Then he built a valve radio.

His house became a huge focal point people listening to music from the airwaves.

This was not all. He built an aeroplane, he went to Dublin and took flying lessons. But there was no one in Ireland that could certify that the plane was safe to fly. He was disapointed but he went on.

There was an empty shop in Carrickmacross and he went to the bank manager to get a loan to open a shop. He wanted to build and repair valve radios.

The manager said NO !

Some time later he went to the USA where he got a job

in a convent as a handyman.

He met a man who was working for NASA and to cut a long story short, he started working for them.

A space engineer I met had worked with him and he told me."That Irishman was I believe a time traveller, you could not explain how he knew the things that he came up with. He worked closely on the design of the space shuttle "Discovery" and when man landed on the moon they put a plaque on the moon and that lads name is on it"

So a big thank you to the Carrickmacross bank manager for saying no.

SAM THE FREEDOM FIGHTER.

I picked him up on Richmond Rd.

Hurry please I have to get to the airport, I have ½ an hour.

I want you to stop on the way at an internet cafe to print my boarding pass.

Come on! there will be no internet cafes open now. Pay the fine and the next time do it the day before. He was going to London and I asked him why he was going there.

I wrote a book and they want to make a film about it.

What is it called?

"Soldier for a summer!" By Sam Najjair. I have bought the book on Kindle and I saw him talking about the total disintegration in the middle east, he is a very clever man.

His mother is Irish and his father had to flee Libya and it was Sams desire to overthrow Ghidaffi and be free to go home.

Sam led the International brigade in Libya, he is one hell of a brave man there is a TV5 documentary which won first prize showing Sam in action.

The advice I gave him about the film was that they should have come to Dublin to meet him, not the other way around.

This is very important, find a lawyer who works in film. Ask that person to protect the integrity of your story;. You would not like to be portrayed as a mad fool and a drunkard.

Once you sign that contract the book might become their property to do what they like with. He thought about it and he was grateful for the ride.

Sam is a guy who will turn up again, his cousin was from Tallaght and he became the Lord mayor of Tripoli.

In a million miles I met thousands of people, I heard storys that would make your hair caurl, just listen and learn.

BRYAN FERRY

Arthur Guinness has been brewing porter here in Dublin since 1759 and in 1999 they celebrated 250 years in business. Free pints and promotions all round.

They had a concert in the Hop store and I picked up this guy who turned out to be Bryan Ferry. I didn't recognise him at the time but what happened in the car will stay with me forever.

He sat in the front passenger seat and his 2 companions were in the back. He spotted my name on the ID, I hope your night is going ok Paul ?

After 10 minutes or so the back seat passenger's phone rang. "Jim, Oh Jim, I am so sorry I got called away urgently and I had no time to call you back to cancel. I know,I know.

I will call you when I am back in London".

Bryan said, I can't believe it.

Paul what do you think is after happening?

He had arranged to meet a guy and he didn't show up he knew that he would not be in London.

He turned around to the back seat passenger.

You knew for over a year that you would be here on this day.

In showbusiness your word is everything.

The shake of a hand means you are totally committed. Its not that this gig is more important than that gig, so you will just allow a poor sod to go in to central London and book a table in a restaurant and just not show up !

This is not acceptable, not ever.

I had planned to do a few gigs with you over the next year, but not now, we are totally finished.

All you have in this life is your reputation.

After this concert I will block your number from my phone, I will tell my friends what you did.

We will push work Jim's way.
It is so sad that you think so little of other people.

I said "Good man" and shook his hand.

It was really good to see that Bryan Ferry held integrity in such high regard.
He really put the other guy back in his place.

JOE ELLIOTT

I just wanted to finish off with this story.

They often say "never meet your heroes"

Joe Elliott of Deff Leopard fame got into the taxi going to the airport and I told him that I was there right back in the day when Windmill lane studios were all the go and all the girls were flocking after him and Bono was not even known of.

'And we are both still standing', he said.

I asked him what it was like to be famous and he told me.' I get well looked after, I will sign autographs until the pen runs out of ink.

I count signing autographs as writing my own pay check.

Restaurants, shows and partys we get free passes to all the time and I have seen the world free of charge. I enjoy preforming with the band and I have a nice home and a nice car as a result.'

I asked him what car he drives and he said a Maserati quattroporte.

'Do you know that that car has a design fault?' I said.

No! tell me.

Ok, when you are on the motorway and there is a slow car in front and you floor the accelerator,does the car splutter and slow down and then take off again? He nodded."All the time"

All the time.

Do you know why this happens?

Go on tell me.

The air filter is blocked!

How do you know this?

"I buy a magazine called Car mechanics and they had a

feature on that car.

To change the air filter you have to take off the front left wheel. Undo the screws of the wheel arch and push the metal panel back, then you put your hand inside and remove the air filter, you have to clean the inside of the housing with a wet cloth and then put in the new filter and put it all back together again.

The garage man is too lazy to do it".

Bloody hell it costs me over £1,000 to have that car serviced. I'll bloody well kill them.

But it is a really nice car Joe, beautiful leather seats and thank you so much for telling me about your life. I really enjoyed that trip,it was really great to meet you at last Joe.

Well I think I enjoyed it more than you he said

The fare is €22 I will give you the superstar discount, just give me €20..

No Paul. Here is a superstar tip for you',

handing me a €50.

Then we gave each other a big bear-hug.

He really is a super person to meet.

So I will leave you. I hope you enjoyed the trip.

ABOUT THE AUTHOR

Paul Malone

 Written in the Covid-19 emergency. A collection of brief meetings which were taken from his Blog. He drove his taxi over a million miles and he met thousands of interesting people along the way.
We hope you enjoy it.

Made in the USA
Monee, IL
08 January 2021